VIOLENCE AND SOCIETY™

DOMESTIC VIOLENCE

HOLLY CEFREY

Rosen
PUBLISHING®

New York

To victims and survivors

Published in 2009 by The Rosen Publishing Group, Inc.
29 East 21st Street, New York, NY 10010

Library of Congress Cataloging-in-Publication Data

Cefrey, Holly.
Domestic violence / Holly Cefrey.—1st ed.
    p.cm.—(Violence and society)
Includes bibliographical references and index.
ISBN-13: 978-1-4042-1794-2 (library binding)
1. Family violence—United States. I. Title.
HV6626.2.C44 2009
362.82'920973—dc22

                                                    2007048347

Manufactured in Malaysia

CONTENTS

Domestic violence can wreck families and end lives. Pictured here are family and friends of Nixzmary Brown, a seven-year-old girl who died in 2006 from domestic violence.

—Brooklyn, New York, January 2006

It was dark. There were bugs and rodents scurrying throughout the room. A tiny girl lay on the floor next to a chair that she was often tied to when punished. Her name was Nixzmary Brown. Her parents called this dark, ugly place "the dirty room." When Nixzmary or her siblings behaved badly, they were locked away in the dirty room. There was a cat litter box to use instead of a toilet; food was withheld until punishment ended.

Nixzmary found herself again on the floor of this room, but this time she was dying. She had been carelessly tossed into the room after being beaten by her stepfather. Cesar Rodriguez would later tell police that it was part of her punishment for being mischievous. Her mother would tell police that she, too, sometimes joined in beating the little girl. Rodriguez does not deny beating the girl and throwing her into the dirty room. He does not, however, claim responsibility for her death, and neither does her mother. He told Associated Press reporters that he has problems controlling his emotions, "It builds up and I hold it all in. I emotionally just burst," he said.

Nixzmary died from a massive injury to her head. From all the evidence, it was the end of a long history of domestic violence. This included being denied food. She weighed less than forty pounds, which is the right weight for a four-year-old. Nixzmary, however, was seven.

According to the *New York Times*, neighbors thought the girl seemed malnourished and undersized. She had missed a lot of school, and when she did come to school, she often showed up with physical injuries, including a black eye. Sometimes she would say her stepfather caused the injuries. Sometimes she would say she fell down and hurt herself. According to CBS News, the abuse was also sexual in nature. Authorities, including teachers and social workers, knew something was wrong, yet no one was able to stop the violence against the little girl.

On her last night, Nixzmary supposedly took a yogurt cup out of the refrigerator, and she supposedly had something to do with the computer printer not working properly. For these reasons, Cesar Rodriguez apparently flew into a violent rage, starting a sequence of events that ended with the death of Nixzmary Brown. Outside the bathroom, Nixzmary's mother and siblings heard the chilling screams and loud bangs. No one, not her mother or any of her five siblings, tried to stop the abuse. No one did anything to prevent the horrific murder of the little girl.

The Aftermath of a Violent Death

Nixzmary Brown's body was publicly displayed during her funeral on January 16, 2006. She was in a pearl white casket. Her face was heavily covered with makeup to hide the bruises. Those at the chapel included hundreds of strangers who came out of sorrow and anger. They lined the streets of the Lower East Side of Manhattan to pay their respects to the murdered girl.

After Nixzmary's burial, reports surfaced claiming that city health workers knew something was wrong in the household. It became clear that her death should have been prevented.

According to the *New York Times*, schoolteachers complained to the Administration for Children's Services (ACS) and other officials that Nixzmary had suspicious bruises and was missing too much school. Following the law, the officials investigated this report. The family refused to answer the phone, and they turned away social workers at the door. At that point, the workers should have obtained a court order to open the home and investigate, but they did not. Nixzmary's black eye had been reported, but the doctor who examined her said that it could have been caused by a fall.

According to *USA Today*, after Nixzmary's death, six ACS workers were suspended or asked to resign. The failure of social services to prevent

Nixzmary Brown was a girl with a vibrant smile. She died on January 11, 2006, after suffering several hours from untreated abuse injuries.

Nixzmary's death caused thousands of other cases to be opened and reviewed. Officials worried that other children, teens, and spouses were possibly undergoing abuse and were not receiving the help they needed. For a brief moment, the issue of domestic violence received the media attention it deserves.

CHAPTER ONE
A Problem Close to Home

D omestic violence, also called domestic abuse, is defined as an encounter between people living in the same household. Child abuse occurs when a child is the victim of domestic violence. When a wife or husband is the victim, it is called spousal abuse. Domestic violence may include physical, sexual, financial, or emotional abuse.

Risk Factors

Domestic violence crosses all lines; anyone could be an abuser and anyone could be a victim. People of different economic, cultural, and educational backgrounds are affected. Men and women, young and old are affected. However, according to the Centers for Disease Control and Prevention (CDC), there are some groups at higher risk than others. Not everyone at risk becomes involved in domestic violence, but chances are higher that at-risk individuals will be affected. Multiple factors combine to create domestic violence. Knowing what these factors are can empower individuals to see where help may be needed, either in one's own family or in the larger community of friends and acquaintances.

Poverty

Factors within the community that contribute to a frequent occurrence of domestic violence include poverty and

A police officer responds to a domestic abuse complaint in Liberty City, a poverty-stricken neighborhood in Miami, Florida.

overcrowding. Living in poverty leads to despair, stress, and a poor sense of one's own value (also called low self-esteem). When these feelings collide with other negative factors, domestic violence is more likely. Poorer communities also lack resources that would normally serve as an outreach and educational guide to show why and how domestic violence is wrong.

Traditional Social Values

In addition to poverty, the family values commonly found in traditional societies increase the risk of domestic violence. Traditional values include the belief that the man alone should financially support the family, be the disciplinarian, and make important decisions. Such beliefs devalue others in the household, making it more likely for men in these societies to become abusive toward their wives and children.

Alcohol and Drug Abuse

There is a clear connection between substance abuse and domestic violence. When drunk or high, substance abusers are more likely to behave aggressively or act in other socially unacceptable ways. In the aftermath, the substance—rather than the person—is often blamed for the violence, making it harder to sort through the problem. Substance abuse and domestic violence may create a vicious cycle. In *The Domestic Violence Sourcebook*, author Dawn Bradley Berry cites studies that show that individuals who grow up in a violent household are twice as likely to abuse drugs when they get older.

Other Factors

Many other factors also contribute to increased risk of domestic violence. If a married couple argues often, and tension is common, it may easily lead to spousal abuse. Divorces or separations are a highly stressful time. Some partners cannot handle the stress of a failing marriage, and they "snap" and become abusive. Also, if a

person has lost money or a job, he or she may have difficulty handling the pressure and become abusive. If a person was raised as a child in a violent home, he or she may initiate violent behavior as an adult. In this way, the next generation is exposed to the same negative behavior, and the pattern of abuse may continue.

Discipline, Punishment, and Domestic Violence

Nixzmary Brown and her siblings (see Introduction) suffered from domestic violence. Their mother and stepfather believed that what they did to the children in their home was a part of discipline. Discipline is the practice of ensuring that people obey rules. In households, parents or guardians set these rules. In society, these rules are set by our legal system.

In discipline, when rules are broken, there are punishments. These punishments are supposed to teach individuals not to break the rule again. Sometimes, however, it's hard to tell whether a punishment for breaking a rule at home is a form of child abuse.

For many years, there was a great debate about spanking or hitting as part of discipline. People who used spanking as punishment believed that it would prevent a child or teen from breaking rules. They believed that pain would cause the child to remember not to do something that was wrong. However, several studies indicate that spanking is not a good way to teach good behavior. According to the Nemours Foundation, a child welfare group, it's more likely that spanking will serve only to make the child scared of the punisher. It will also encourage the child to try harder to hide the bad behavior, which he or she will probably continue to do despite the spanking. The

Domestic Violence

Spanking or hitting a child has long been a way for parents to discipline for bad behavior. It was believed that children would behave better to avoid getting spanked again.

American Academy of Pediatrics warns that spanking and hitting also teach children that it's OK to be physically aggressive when upset.

Human-rights agencies and committees such as the Global Initiative to End All Corporal Punishment of Children are working to end spanking and hitting as punishment altogether. They believe that since adults are taught not to hit other adults, then they shouldn't be hitting their children. They believe there are much better ways to train a young person to follow rules and laws.

Smarter, Safer Punishment and Discipline

Sometimes, the disciplinarian—the person who makes and enforces rules—is your mother or father. Sometimes it's a foster parent. Sometimes it's an aunt, uncle, or older sibling. If your guardian is using physical means to make you follow the rules, you need to have a discussion about what will really make you follow rules. If your guardian is unwilling to calmly discuss the issue, consult the resources at the back of this book or tell one of your teachers, a counselor, a religious leader, or another trusted adult. Whatever you may have done, hitting is not a valid disciplinary solution.

Be aware that in your teen years, you may get aggressive during arguments over rules and punishments. You may raise

your voice, or your parent may become angry because he or she is frustrated. During these "heated" exchanges, both you and your parent need to keep a safe physical distance (five feet or more) from each other. Ask if you can talk about it when you are both calm. Remind your parent that you make mistakes like everybody else, and you'd like to talk about it when you are no longer upset.

Types of Abuse

Domestic violence occurs in homes. It is a behavior that a person uses to gain power and control over another person in a relationship. The most common forms of domestic violence involved in child abuse as well as spousal or partner abuse are physical, emotional, financial, and sexual abuse, and neglect.

Physical abuse is any harm that a person does to another person's body. The abuser knowingly uses force to cause pain. Physical abuse includes hitting, bumping, pushing, pinching, slapping, punching, squeezing, and shaking. It can include the use of objects, such as burning cigarettes on the skin. Many domestic abusers inflict (cause) pain in areas that are covered by clothing. They do this so that the bruises are hidden and the abuse remains a secret.

Emotional abuse is also known as psychological abuse. "Psychological" means relating to the mind. This abuse is not physical; it is mental. An emotional abuser says mean things to, insults, harasses, threatens, or intimidates (creates fear in) a victim. This type of abuse causes the victim to feel scared, nervous, and isolated.

Financial or economic abuse is withholding certain things so that a person is dependent upon the withholder. Victims are powerless to obtain these things for themselves, so they must

Corporal Punishment

Physical acts such as spanking, hitting, or slapping are also known as corporal punishment. "Corporal" means relating to the body. Parents who believe in corporal punishment may use a variety of techniques beyond simply spanking. They include pinching, shaking, punching, slapping, kicking, and beating. Spankers may also use objects like belts, brushes, wooden utensils, cords, or ropes. According to the Center for the Improvement of Child Caring, all such acts are considered violence. They are acts carried out against another with the intention to cause physical pain or injury.

With all violence, there is a victim. If you've been disciplined with corporal punishment, the victim is you. Your suffering doesn't end with the hit. According to the Clinical Child and Family Psychology Review, there are symptoms that continue to affect a victim of corporal violence, even after any physical wounds have healed. They are:

- Depression or thoughts of suicide
- Tendency to strike younger siblings or peers
- Poor performance at school
- More serious violation of the rules
- Urge to commit crimes
- Developing into an abusive parent later on

If you have any of these symptoms, it's time to get help. Your parents or guardians may not understand the effects their actions are having on you. Talk to a relative, teacher, counselor, or religious leader. It's time to change things so that you are given rules and punishments that make sense, and your parent is given a new way to cope with frustration.

beg the withholder for help. A financial abuser might make someone else in the household do illegal things for money. The abuser might also take child support checks or money and spend it on himself or herself rather than on the person it was intended to help.

Sexual abuse occurs when a person touches another person inappropriately, in a sexual area or in a sexual way. Touching in a sexual way can range from a "massage" that goes too far to rape, which is forced sexual intercourse. Sexual abuse also includes being exposed to items or images of an explicit or sexual nature, such as pornography.

Neglect describes a failure to take care of another because of thoughtlessness or carelessness. Things that everyone needs are food, water, shelter, clothing, and personal hygiene. A person who neglects another may not be providing some or all of these things. Neglect can also be emotional. Abusers may avoid hugging, touching, or saying kind words. Many who fail to properly care for their children or partners are under the influence of drugs or alcohol, as the substance abuse changes their ideas of what is important.

Who Are the Victims?

The victims of domestic violence come in all shapes and sizes. They can be big and strong, or small and weak. Wealthy, poor, well educated, or poorly educated, it doesn't matter. Anyone can be a victim. If you or your siblings, parents, or grandparents are victims of domestic violence, you are not alone. The back of this book lists organizations for help, and for immediate help you can call:

The things we say or do not say to loved ones can be abuse. An abuser may say harsh things or threaten you, or he or she may not say anything comforting or loving at all.

National Domestic Violence Hotline: 800-799-SAFE (800-799-7233), TTY: 800-787-3224
Childhelp USA: 800-4-A-CHILD (800-422-4453)

Victims of Child Abuse

Children may be victimized by parents, grandparents, guardians, or older siblings. Boys and girls are victimized at similar rates. According to the Nemours Foundation, both girls and boys

experience all forms of domestic violence, but boys are beaten more often than girls.

The Administration on Children and Families is part of the U.S. Department of Health and Human Services. Detailed reports published by this administration in 2007 state that an estimated 899,000 children across the United States were victims of child abuse in 2005. About 60 percent of these children were victims of neglect. More than 16 percent were physically abused; and almost 10 percent were sexually abused.

Victims of Spousal Abuse and Partner Abuse

Spousal abuse occurs between husbands and wives. Dating or partner abuse occurs between unmarried romantic partners. According to U.S. Department of Justice (DOJ) statistics, the incidence of spousal and partner abuse has been in decline since 1993. However, these types of abuse are still all too common. A DOJ study published in 2005 says that more than 1.7 million violent crimes are committed every year by one spouse against another.

DOJ studies have found that those who report spousal and partner abuse are most often women. Between 1998 and 2002, for example, 84 percent of spouse abuse victims were females, and 86 percent of victims of dating or partner abuse were females. The most recent DOJ statistics state that females between twenty and twenty-four years of age are at the greatest risk for dating or partner violence.

Many men (and women, too) are victims of stalking, which is a form of emotional abuse. According to the American Academy of Family Physicians, about 371,000 men are stalked or menaced by partners or former partners each year.

Domestic abuse can be harder to hide as abuse continues. If someone you know has mysterious bruises, it's time to seek help from a counselor or trusted adult.

Victims of Elder Abuse

The National Center on Elder Abuse says that in 2005, between one and two million elders may have been victims of domestic abuse. Older victims may be abused by their adult children or by workers in assisted living homes. According to the Mayo Clinic, people over the age of eighty are at the greatest risk for this type of abuse because they are less likely to say anything about the abuse.

CHAPTER TWO

Recognizing Abusers and Abuse

T he behaviors of domestic violence have direct results. The abuser's behaviors harm victims emotionally, physically, and spiritually. Abusive behaviors frighten, intimidate, manipulate, humiliate, terrorize, and wound a person, and not just while it's happening, but for life. These behaviors do not happen by accident. They are tactics, or activities planned to bring about an expected end. In both child abuse and spousal abuse, the abuser wants the victim to feel frightened, intimidated, manipulated, humiliated, terrorized, or wounded. Abusers have a need to feel power and control over victims.

Who Are the Abusers?

There is no single type of person who becomes a domestic abuser. You can't look at someone and tell whether he or she is an abuser. According to a report published by the U.S. Department of Health and Human Services in 2004, about 58 percent of child abusers were women and 42 percent were men. According to the National Center for Victims of Crime, there are a few common characteristics that most abusers share. Many have Jekyll-and-Hyde-type personalities. Outside of the home, the abuser seems happy and nonaggressive. Household members however, see the other side, which is often spiteful and cruel. Many abusers suffer from mood

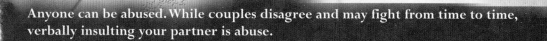

Anyone can be abused. While couples disagree and may fight from time to time, verbally insulting your partner is abuse.

swings, meaning they are high and happy one moment, and sad or depressed the next.

Most abusers have low self-esteem. Your self-esteem is the way you value yourself as a human being. Abusers often need to feel power and control over others in order to build their self-esteem. A lot of abusers developed low self-esteem because they were raised in homes with domestic violence. They have learned abusive behaviors that allow them to feel powerful over others. They have seen loved ones stay with abusers, which confuses the issue of whether it is wrong or right. They have seen how violent acts get results for others, so they develop the belief that it's OK to use violence to get things for themselves.

Both child abusers and spousal abusers become practiced at controlling victims by offering a period of peace and happiness. After a violent outburst, an abuser may be loving and regretful for several days. He or she may give the victim gifts and promise to seek help. This lulls victims into thinking the violence won't happen again. Unfortunately, without help, it usually does.

Why Abuse Happens

People who grow up in abusive homes are more likely to become abusers. Not all people raised in violent homes will definitely become abusive. It just means that they are more inclined or open to having certain thoughts about violence. Ultimately, it is up to the individual to break the cycle of violence by finding other ways to cope with frustration.

Many abusers have difficulty managing their feelings. If they get angry, they scream and throw things. Blowing up is a quick,

The Abuser Profile

A 2001 study published by researchers at the Oregon Social Learning Center in Eugene stated that parents who were neglected or abused in childhood are significantly more likely to neglect or abuse their own children. More recent studies, including one conducted at the University of Texas at Austin and published in 2006, confirm this claim. The pattern of abuse varies depending on the individual case, but there is now little doubt that people raised around domestic violence are more likely to become abusers later in life. If you were raised to think that hitting, beating, shoving, and yelling are a natural part of anger, you may think they are normal. However, it isn't healthy to want to cause another person pain. Seek help from your guidance counselor if you recognize abusive tendencies within yourself.

A person is an abuser if he or she:

- Controls the finances so another person has to beg for necessities like food
- Controls another person's life so he or she is isolated (keeps the person from going to school, work, or out with others)
- Controls another person's life so he or she cannot make independent decisions
- Acts in ways against another in order to scare him or her
- Acts jealous or possessive and makes paranoid accusations about another person
- Calls another person names and insults him or her
- Is physically aggressive (hits, kicks, pushes, chokes, or uses objects or weapons to inflict pain)

- Forces another to take part in sexual acts against his or her will

An abuser might also:

- Become abusive when drinking liquor or taking drugs
- Act suicidal (make risky decisions that could end his or her life)
- Destroy objects and property
- Blame the victim for the violence, stating he or she deserves it
- Deny having done any violent activity
- Take aggressive action to keep victims from getting help, such as threatening to kill victims

Alcohol and drugs can alter behavior. Gentle people can suddenly become aggressive. Seek help if someone you know becomes abusive when drinking.

Watching your parents fight can be scary. Don't get in between your parents when they fight. Talk to a trusted adult if the fights are frequent or abusive.

easy release, but the problem doesn't go away. Nothing is solved by these actions, and the hard-to-manage feelings remain bubbling beneath the surface.

You can manage your feelings by developing coping skills and self-discipline. When something happens that upsets us, we use our past experiences to react to current problems. People with good coping skills remember that blowing up didn't solve anything. Instead, they solve problems by looking within to try to understand their thoughts, motivations, behaviors, and feelings. Then they discipline themselves to act differently.

Many abusers blame stress for their outbursts. Adult abusers face financial, work, and relationship stress. If they do not have an outlet, such as exercise, therapy, or hobbies, the stress may build until something bad happens and pushes them over the edge. Stress may be a lot to cope with, but it is never an excuse to abuse someone.

Another reason why domestic violence occurs is because the abuser is abusing other things, such as alcohol or drugs. These substances impair judgment as well as the ability to control feelings and actions. Abusers may be intoxicated or drunk and therefore don't realize they are being violent or manipulative. If you know an abuser who is a substance abuser as well, tell a trusted adult so that this person can get the help he or she needs to heal.

Domestic Violence Is a Crime

You may have gotten into an argument with your mother, father, or sibling, and you were hit. Maybe you told yourself that it was an accident and forgot about it. If it happens again, you may overlook it again, especially if everything seems to snap right back to a peaceful lull. Maybe you have watched your parents arguing all your life and don't realize that when your father hits your mother—or vice versa—it's domestic violence. You and anyone else suffering with you may be thinking such treatment is normal and deserved. This is an example of how low self-esteem causes a victim to lose sight of what's right and wrong. The fact is domestic violence is a crime. According to the American Bar Association, domestic violence is considered a crime in all states. The legal system recognizes all domestic abuse forms as possible crime-related activity.

A man beats a woman in this fifteenth-century German drawing. Prior to the twentieth century, women had few legal protections against domestic violence.

Prosecuting Spousal and Partner Abuse

The National Center for Victims of Crime states that spousal abuse is part of human history, dating back to our earliest written records. According to the book *Domestic Violence and Healthcare: What Every Professional Needs to Know*, men of ancient times were expected to control their wives

through physical and emotional means. Ancient Egyptian husbands were encouraged to use weapons against their wives if the women spoke out against them. Later, during the Middle Ages, English men could physically punish their wives with little fear of negative consequences.

In the twentieth century, with the widespread increase in women's rights, violence against partners became a crucial topic.

Demonstrators carry cardboard images representing victims of domestic violence. The march was held in South Carolina on October 29, 1997, to call attention to the issue of domestic violence.

Women have gradually gained more power in the household. Along with this power has come more negotiation and less violence. In many progressive communities, abusive tactics have largely been replaced by mutual respect between partners and greater peace in the household. While this is a favorable development, domestic violence is still a global issue.

In the United States, complaints arising from spousal and partner abuse are handled by the police and courts, not social service agencies. These complaints may result in misdemeanor charges being filed against the abuser. In most states, once charges are filed, a judge may order the abuser to stay away from the victim and his or her children, or even order the abuser to leave the home. If an abuser desires to be reunited with his or her family, the courts may require him or her to undergo abuse counseling or an intervention program.

Child Abuse and the Law

Unlike spousal abuse complaints, child abuse complaints are handled not by the police but by child protection agencies or other social service agencies. As a result, child abuse rarely results in criminal prosecution. Unfortunately, social service agencies are often stretched too thin to be effective all of the time. Many who need help because of domestic violence may not get it in a timely manner, or they may be forced to go without it altogether.

Individuals involved in health and social services typically work on dozens of cases in a week. They must follow strict regulations on investigating reports, but they must be sure not to trample on individual rights or make false accusations. If someone is wrongfully charged with child abuse, the state may be sued, causing further loss of resources.

If caseworkers were less burdened, there would be a better chance that claims could be properly investigated. Unburdening our local services is a matter of politics. To improve your local system, individuals in the community have to tell their civic leaders that domestic violence is a problem for which a solution must be sought. Organizations such as the National Coalition Against Domestic Violence (NCADV) offer several resources for getting your community into the process.

Myth: Domestic violence is a private family matter that is best kept private.

Fact: Domestic violence has become a very public matter. Major corporations, including Liz Claiborne, Marshall's, Polaroid, and the Body Shop, are using their corporate resources to develop campaigns and public awareness programs. The only way to end domestic violence is to make secrets public and to bring in help from outside of the family unit that is suffering.

Myth: Women and children are the victims of domestic violence.

Fact: Anyone, including adult men, can be a victim of domestic violence, and no one deserves it. Studies have shown that men are just as likely as women to suffer domestic abuse.

Myth: Abuse is obvious; a person knows when he or she is being abused.

Fact: Some types of nonphysical domestic abuse are very subtle, or hard to recognize. For instance, a parent may abuse a child by making the child say things to the other parent that the child doesn't want to say. In this case, nobody is physically injured, but the emotional and psychological damage this causes is a form of domestic abuse that should not be tolerated.

Taking Action Against Domestic Violence

NCADV offers a complete Legislative Action Guide on its Web site (http://www.ncadv.org). This guide offers sample letters and actions that you can do in your community to reduce domestic violence. The coalition also provides resources for victims and survivors of domestic violence, as well as sponsors twelve national awareness conferences around the country.

Two women talk on the front porch of a battered women's shelter. Shelters are places to go for guidance on leaving a bad situation and when you feel you have nowhere else to turn.

A Place to Go

Many of the major strides taken against violence in the home have occurred since the first women's domestic violence shelter was built, in 1974. Shelters for battered women and families are found spread across the United States. Shelters are buildings or apartments that offer temporary lodging and support for women and other victims of domestic violence. A staff runs the shelter, operating around the clock. It's common for staff members to be former victims.

People who resort to shelters need to be emotionally healed, and their self-esteem needs to be boosted to show them that they don't deserve their current fate. Victims fleeing financial domestic abusers often need time to hone their job skills and find a job in order to live independently.

Victims also need to be educated on their legal rights. Each state has its own laws and systems to deal with domestic violence. Shelters within each state can give immediate counseling on the right actions to take to break out of domestic violence.

Shelters try to protect the identity of their guests. They maintain secrecy so that abusers cannot track down their victims. When a victim goes to a shelter, she or he does not have to give a real name. This allows the victim to get away from the abuser, get established, and get on to a safer life. Shelters provide food and clothing to those who need it. As victims get back on their feet, counselors at the shelter may help find them a new home and job. Resources for individual states can be found at the U.S. Department of Health and Human Service Web site, at http://www.womenshealth.gov/violence/state.

CHAPTER THREE

Putting an End to Domestic Violence

Y ou've probably heard the expression, "Kids are growing up too fast." This expression implies that young people today have to face a lot of tough, grown-up subjects. Domestic violence is one of these subjects.

Unfortunately for victims, the typical cycle of domestic violence doesn't come to an end because something changes within the abuser. Something else has to happen. For instance, the end of the cycle may come when the victim or a friend of the victim "blows the whistle" and breaks the secret. On the other hand, the cycle of violence may end on a tragic note, with the serious injury or even death of the victim. When it comes to interrupting the cycle of domestic violence, steps taken early on may make all the difference in the outcome. If you are confronting domestic violence, this means that you may have to do the grown-up thing, the brave thing, and be the one to effect change.

There are things your whole family can do during the good times, when you do not feel threatened. There are things you can do if it's not you but a friend who's being abused. There are things you can do if your boyfriend or girlfriend is abusing you. There are also things you can do if one of your parents is always the abuse victim, yet you remain unscathed.

In any situation, it's very important to remember that the victim of domestic violence does not deserve it. Whether the victim spilled a drink, looked at another person in a funny

Daily stresses can test family relationships. When you disagree or argue with your parents or guardians, try to remain calm and request that your guardian remain calm, too.

way, or even wrecked the family car, he or she does not deserve to be abused.

Steps to Ending Violence

According to the Mayo Clinic, abuse tends to get worse, more frequent, and more violent as it continues. The periods between the abuse also become shorter. Abuse disorients people, leaving

them lost and confused. Victims may start to feel like all the abuse is their fault, and that they just need to learn how to make the abuser happy. As a part of this process, victims learn about the triggers that make the abuser start the abuse. They then live their lives trying to avoid those triggers. It's not their life anymore, but their abuser's to control.

If you have been victimized so often that you know your abuser's triggers, it's time to get immediate help. This type of

10 QUESTIONS TO ASK Yourself

Is your parent, partner, or sibling:

1. Calling you names and criticizing you?

2. Punishing you by withholding affection and kindness?

3. Threatening to hurt you?

4. Forcing you to do things that make you feel uncomfortable?

5. Making you *do* uncomfortable things for money?

6. Preventing you from talking about certain problems at home?

7. Forcing you to do sexual things?

8. Holding you captive at home?

9. Keeping you from eating, drinking, or taking care of necessities?

10. Using physical force against you?

violence or abuse isn't going to stop without an intervention. It's time to create an action plan for putting a stop to the undesirable situation.

Intervention

The first step is to call the abuse what it is: domestic violence. If a friend or family member is being abused, help her or him to see that it's abuse. Tell her or him your view of how it looks from the outside. Victims are often paralyzed by fear or confusion. Seeing it through your eyes might help to snap the victim out of the daze. Be encouraging because any harsh talk may just add to the shame and fear. Tell your friend that you think she or he is an amazing, strong person. Make it clear that you're there to offer support when your friend decides that she or he is ready to leave. Remind your friend that leaving the abuser isn't abandonment. It is taking a big step toward a healthier life.

Ask for outside help. Tell your parents (if abused by a boyfriend, girlfriend, or sibling), a friend, a teacher, a guidance counselor, a doctor, or a trusted relative. Tell someone what is going on so that the burden is not all on you. It's OK to need help; you're not weak if you ask for help. You're actually making a brave, strong decision.

If your abuser has already made promises to get help, approach him or her during a calm period, and ask if it's OK to talk about that promise. If the abuse involves other family members, have them nearby for support. Have a friend waiting outside for you just in case things go badly. If you sense that the abuser is upset with the situation, calmly say that it's not a big deal and switch the subject. End the discussion soon thereafter so that a problem doesn't arise. Now you'll have

Sometimes we need to seek guidance and support from people other than our household members. Doing so, when faced with domestic violence, can save your life.

given the abuser a chance to make the change first—and it wasn't taken.

The Safety Plan

When confronted, an abuser can have unpredictable responses. A safety plan is important for the victim's health and well-being. A safety plan is a plan of action to take when it's time to leave. Being prepared helps the victim leave without hesitation and just may save a life. The victim is not betraying the abusive parent, guardian, partner, sibling, or relative by leaving. He or she is helping the abuser face facts. Just as someone would avoid other uncomfortable situations in life, a rational person wants to avoid abuse.

If it is a friend who is being abused, tell him or her to make your family a part of the safety plan. Let your friend know that he or she can count on your family for transportation to a shelter or if he or she needs a house to run to in troubled times to call 911. If your friend cannot leave the house, work out a signal so that you'll know whether to call the police. As an alternative, your friend could arrange to send a younger brother or sister to your house to alert you.

Victims looking to leave their abusive home should create an emergency bag. Pack it with a change of clothes, money, keys, medications, a flashlight, and telephone numbers of friends, relatives, teachers, the local sheriff's office, and the local shelter. The emergency bag should have the number of the National Domestic Violence Hotline (NDVH), too: (800) 799-7233. Victims can even call the hotline now to alert them that they are making a safety plan and need to know about local resources. Pack a map

The Web has hundreds of resources that can help you sort through the confusing issues related to domestic violence. The National Domestic Violence Hotline site (www.ndvh.org) helps empower victims.

of the escape route. If transportation is needed, call the shelter or the sheriff's office.

If you know of an elder who is being abused, call local welfare services. They will investigate. If you suspect that your grandparent is being abused at a nursing home, file a complaint with the manager and your state's long-term-care ombudsman.

Emergency 911

Many victims know that certain acts or words will cause an abuser to start abuse tactics. Some situations may become emergencies. Any time an abuser is hitting, choking, or using a weapon against a victim, it's an emergency situation.

In these cases, call 911 immediately. It is better to have the police arrive to break up the disturbance than hope that it goes away by itself. Even if things are calm by the time the police arrive, at least they will have a record of the disturbance. Other actions to take:

- Stay away from small rooms or a bathroom where you could get trapped.
- Stay away from the kitchen and a closed garage, where there are things that can be used as weapons against you.
- Move toward a room that has a door or window from which you can escape.
- If you can't escape, get to a room where you can call 911.
- Run to a neighbor's or a friend's house to get help.
- Know where the local shelter is ahead of time, so when you run, you have a place to go immediately.
- If someone else is being attacked, do not get in the middle of the fight. Immediately call 911 or go to a neighbor's house for help.

As soon as the police arrive, tell the officer(s) everything that happened. If there is a history of abuse, tell the officer. Show any signs of abuse, whether they be on your body, another victim's body, or broken furniture or walls. Take pictures of every bruise or injury.

Domestic disturbance calls can be tricky for police. Oftentimes, abused spouses may confront officers while they are questioning or arresting the reported abuser. These officers are trained for such cases.

You can call the NDVH or your local adult protective services agency to get immediate assistance.

Control of Information

Abusers take steps to maintain the control. A major element of control is keeping track of victims' communications. Financial abusers may limit their victims' time outside with others. They may deprive victims of standard modes of communication, such as the phone or computer. Abusers may check cell phone histories, trace calls, or monitor computer use. Victims should keep a journal regarding the abuse so that when the time comes, they will have evidence of a history of abuse.

Victims can use outside resources, such as a school's or a friend's computer, when creating a safety plan. If a victim is captive at home but has access to a computer, he or she can sign up for a free Web-based e-mail account. (Gmail, Yahoo!, and Hotmail are examples.) E-mails sent and received using these accounts are stored on the company's mail server and not on the local computer. This may keep an abuser from finding out that the victim is actively looking for help. Victims can also use the Help section of their Web browsers to learn how to erase their Web history, if they don't already know how. Then they should erase their history after every session. Regaining control of the ability to communicate with others is an important step in breaking the domestic violence cycle.

CHAPTER FOUR

Victims Take Back the Power

Exiting an abusive domestic situation is not easy. Many cases need to involve social workers as well as police and other law enforcement officials. It isn't easy for a victim to go public with a family or relationship secret, but it may be necessary to save lives. Any abuse—financial, emotional, sexual, physical, neglect—can lead to generations of pain if not treated. As a victim, your connection with a domestic abuser who is a relative will last a lifetime. You're not ending your relationship by exposing the abuse. You're ending the part of your life that kept you from experiencing healthy, well-adjusted happiness. Abusers who decide to change and become healthy rarely hate the individuals who sought help. If they do, they still haven't healed. Victims cannot worry about losing their abuser's love.

What Happens When You Tell?

In their attempts to get help, victims may find that people are shocked. Remember, a common characteristic of domestic abusers is that they are perfectly charming in public. The abusive side is their secret they hide at home. When you are a victim of domestic abuse and you tell your teacher, friend, relative, parent, or doctor, this individual may circle back to your abuser to confront him or her. If you are fearful for your safety, ask this person not to confront your abuser.

When you are a victim of domestic violence, or you love someone who is, your whole life is affected. School, work, and relationships are harder while you face this tough issue.

If a victim calls the police, a report will be filed, and the abuser may be taken to jail, depending on the nature of the abuse. If an abused parent calls the police, she or he may press charges or seek to have the abusing partner removed from the house altogether. It's okay if this happens. The break may be what the abusive parent needs in order to get help. A public outing typically forces the abuser to learn better, nonviolent ways of dealing with family and stress. During this confusing time, it's important for everyone involved to start speaking with a counselor. This person can help everyone involved to feel good about the decision that was made and to deal with the dramatic changes that are likely to take place.

If a teacher is involved, he or she may already be trained to handle domestic violence. Most teachers are required by law to report incidents of suspected domestic abuse. In response to the report, a social worker will come to investigate the complaint.

Dating Violence

Domestic violence also occurs in dating relationships. Our choice in a romantic partner can bring out the best or the worst in each of us. Through relationships, we learn new things about ourselves. You may discover that you feel jealous or protective of your partner. While jealousy is a common emotion, it is not healthy. It suggests that the person feeling it does not trust his or her partner. It also suggests a hidden need to control another person.

A young individual who is capable of abuse is capable of abusing a future spouse, child, or elder. If you are dating someone who you think has abusive tendencies, seek help. You'll set your partner on a better path, which can lead to a long, happy relationship. No one is perfect, but no one should settle for an abuser.

Is Your Relationship Heading for Trouble?

Certain signs may indicate that your romantic relationship may be affected by abuse. If the following statements describe your relationship, speak to someone about it so that you and your partner can get counseling.

You and/or your partner:

- Need to be with the other all the time
- Need to know what the other is doing all the time
- Make attempts to be the primary focus of the other's life, above family, work, friends, and school
- Get jealous seeing the other talk with someone else
- Feel angry when not enough attention is paid to the relationship
- Pressure the other into doing uncomfortable things
- Had a whirlwind, fast bond almost instantly

Romantic relationships may involve sexual relations, but they should never involve sexual abuse. Addressing this issue doesn't mean it's the end of your relationship. It just means that you're going to try to get it repaired. If you're experiencing any of the following, talk to a guidance counselor, trusted friend, or relative immediately.

Your partner:

- Thinks women are sex objects and believes deeply in male-female gender roles
- Insists that you dress in a "sexy" way
- Tells you you're unattractive
- Forces you to perform sexual acts against your will
- Tells you your feelings about sex are wrong

Romantic relationships may include arguments and fights. However, if your health and safety are threatened, you need to change the nature of your relationship right away.

The Painful Aftermath of Abuse

Victims of abuse go through trauma. Trauma is a stressful experience that causes severe emotional shock, which may have long-lasting mental effects. There are well-known conditions that go along with trauma. Anyone who has been the victim of domestic abuse should seek counseling, even if only for one session. Speaking to a counselor at school or work can lighten

the heavy burden you may feel as a result of the abuse you suffered, witnessed, or caused.

According to the American Psychiatric Association, domestic violence can trigger mental illness. Abused individuals often suffer from depression, anxiety, and panic attacks. During a panic attack, one feels an extremely powerful, immobilizing paranoia (the feeling that people are "out to get you"). Younger victims might become more aggressive. They may lack self-esteem, become shy, or have difficulty at school. They may think about committing suicide. Victims may suffer from a condition know as post-traumatic stress disorder (PTSD). This disorder causes difficulties such as high anxiety, depression, fatigue (low energy), and flashbacks.

These symptoms may cause victims to have difficulty thinking and functioning normally. They may come to have a very poor self-image, or have extreme difficulty in trusting people. Other symptoms include:

- Trouble eating and sleeping
- Difficulty concentrating
- Nightmares
- Feelings of shame
- Socially withdrawing from friends, family, and favorite activities
- Feelings of hopelessness
- Feeling numb

If you or someone you know is suffering with these symptoms, it's time to see a doctor, therapist, or counselor. Victims may need medication to get through the initial phases

You may feel as though you are alone and no one else understands your situation. Isolating yourself only adds to your continued suffering.

of recovery from abuse. There are also nonmedical relaxation and exercise techniques that a doctor may recommend.

There is no shame in suffering from these symptoms. They are a normal part of responding to treatment that the victim didn't deserve. Victims should not feel as though they have to hide these symptoms from others. Symptoms exist for a reason: they tell us what's wrong so that we become aware that something needs to be fixed.

Domestic Violence Traps

The most important part of breaking the cycle of violence is making sure that the victim is healed. Victims may never be able to forget what they witnessed or experienced, but they don't have to let the violence stay with them throughout their lives. Working through the memories and experiences—while they can be just as painful as the original abuse—is crucial to victims' healthy futures. If someone you love is a victim, try to get him or her into counseling so that healing can begin.

It is crucial that recovering victims face their issues without resorting to substance abuse. Many victims of domestic violence turn to drugs and alcohol. They believe they can numb the pain of the memories or quiet the symptoms. This is not a healthy solution. When they sober up, they realize the memory and the pain are still there, and they haven't healed at all. Substance abuse only delays the healing process. Some recovering victims may become "cutters" who punish themselves. Cutters inflict cuts on their skin. This is a type of self-abuse called self-mutilation. Any abuse that you inflict upon yourself is an alternative that does not produce healing.

When you take the brave steps of ending the cycle of violence, healing can begin. Life is better when your future holds the promise of domestic peace.

Victims often blame themselves for what happened. If you are a victim, don't fall into this trap. You did not deserve the abuse, and you do not deserve the aftermath. You may think that if you try to forget what happened, everything will be fine. This is not a healthy solution either. A little bit of denial is good because it helps an individual get through rough memories or experiences that would normally harm the human mind. Denial should not be a long-term solution. Remaining in denial and not facing the truth of what happened will keep you locked as the victim and will keep you from becoming the survivor. Take steps to become a survivor. Seek help and see a better future far away from the abuse that you or someone you know has experienced.

anxiety Painful feeling of uneasiness.

assault Violent physical or verbal attack.

coalition Combination or alliance of organizations working toward a common goal.

confrontational Seeking a face-to-face encounter or meeting.

corporal Relating or belonging to the body.

deprive To take something away from.

discipline Practice of ensuring that people obey rules.

disorient To cause someone to feel lost or confused.

explicit Openly portraying nudity or sexual activity.

impair To lessen the strength of something.

incidence Rate of occurrence.

inflict To cause to be endured.

intentional Done on purpose, not by accident.

intervention Action that is taken to put a stop to something undesirable.

intimidate To create a feeling of fear in another person.

intoxicated Drunk.

introspective Describing one who looks inward to understand one's thoughts, motivations, behaviors, and feelings.

manipulate To control by unfair means to serve one's purpose.

neglect To disregard; to give little attention to.

ombudsman Government official appointed to receive and investigate complaints, often against other government officials or organizations.

pornography Pictures or writing intended to cause sexual excitement.

psychological Relating to the mind; mental.

self-esteem Confidence a person has in himself or herself as a valuable human being.

self-mutilation Act of deliberately injuring oneself.

spousal Describing the relationship between a wife and husband.

stalking Pursuing or following someone stealthily. Stalking is a form of emotional abuse.

tactics Planned activities to bring about an expected aim.

trauma Stressful experience that causes severe emotional shock, which may have long-lasting mental effects.

unscathed Unharmed.

The Battered Women's Justice Project
2104 4th Avenue South, Suite B
Minneapolis, MN 55404
(800) 903-0111, ext. 1 or (612) 824-8768
Web site: http://www.bwjp.org
This organization offers training, technical assistance, and consultation
on the most promising practices of the criminal and civil justice system
in addressing domestic violence.

Canadian Health Network: Violence Prevention
Public Health Agency of Canada
Jeanne Mance Building, 10th Floor
Tunney's Pasture, AL 1910B
Ottawa, ON K1A 0K9
Canada
E-mail: chn-info-rcs@phac-aspc.gc.ca
Web site: http://www.canadian-health-network.ca
This government agency site provides information, links, and further
resources on domestic violence for all of Canada.

Faith Trust Institute (formerly Center for the Prevention of
    Sexual and Domestic Violence)
2400 North 45th Street, #10
Seattle, WA 98103
(206) 634-1903
E-mail: info@faithtrustinstitute.org
Web site: http://www.faithtrustinstitute.org
FaithTrust Institute is a multifaith organization that offers services and
resources including training, consultation, and educational materials to
end sexual and domestic violence.

Family Violence Prevention Fund
383 Rhode Island Street, Suite 304
San Francisco, CA 94103-5133
(415) 252-8900
E-mail: info@endabuse.org
Web site: http://www.endabuse.org
This organization strives to prevent violence within the home, and in the community, to help those whose lives are devastated by violence, because everyone has the right to live free of violence.

National Coalition Against Domestic Violence
1120 Lincoln Street, Suite 1603
Denver, CO 80203
(303) 839-1852
Web site: http://www.ncadv.org
This organization serves as a national information and referral center for the general public, media, battered women and their children, and allied and member agencies and organizations.

National Council on Child Abuse and Family Violence
1025 Connecticut Avenue NW, Suite 1000
Washington, DC 20036
(800) 222-2000 or (202) 429-6695
E-mail: info@nccafv.org
Web site: http://www.nccafv.org
This council offers violence prevention services by bringing together community and national stakeholders, professionals, and volunteers to prevent domestic violence (spouse/partner abuse), child abuse, and elder abuse.

National Domestic Violence Hotline
(800) 799-SAFE (7233)

Text telephone: (800) 787-3224

Web site: http://www.ndvh.org

This is a toll-free helpline, available 24 hours a day, 365 days a year. It is for victims and anyone calling on their behalf to provide crisis intervention, safety planning, information, and referrals to agencies in all fifty states and Puerto Rico.

National Network to End Domestic Violence

2001 South Street NW, Suite 400

Washington, DC 20009

(202) 543-5566

Web site: http://www.nnedv.org

The network works to understand the ongoing and emerging needs of domestic violence victims and advocacy programs. People in the network communicate their findings to lawmakers and community leaders.

National Resource Center on Domestic Violence

Pennsylvania Coalition Against Domestic Violence

6400 Flank Drive, Suite 1300

Harrisburg, PA 17112

(800) 537-2238

Text telephone: (800) 553-2508

Web site: http://www.nrcdv.org

This organization provides information and resources, policy development, and technical assistance designed to enhance community response to and prevention of domestic violence.

National Teen Dating Abuse Helpline (NTDAH)

(866) 331-9474

Text telephone: 866-331-8453

Web site: http://www.loveisrespect.org

Domestic Violence

Part of the Liz Claiborne Corporation, this is a twenty-four-hour national Web-based and telephone resource for teens (ages thirteen to eighteen) who are experiencing dating abuse, serving all fifty states, Puerto Rico, and the Virgin Islands.

Rape Abuse and Incest National Network (RAINN)
2000 L Street NW, Suite 406
Washington, DC 20036
(202) 544-1034
Hotline: (800) 656-HOPE (4673)
E-mail: info@rainn.org
Web site: http://www.rainn.org
RAINN is a nationwide partnership of more than 1,100 local rape treatment hotlines that provides victims of sexual assault with free, confidential services around the clock.

Resource Center on Domestic Violence, Child Protection, and
     Custody (NCJFCJ)
P.O. Box 8970
Reno, NV 89507
(775) 784-6012 or (800) 527-3223
E-mail: staff@ncjfcj.org
This is a network that improves courts and systems practice and raises awareness of the core issues that touch the lives of many of our nation's children and families.

Safe Horizon
2 Lafayette Street, 3rd Floor
New York, NY 10007
(212) 577-7700
Hotline: (800) 621-HOPE (4673)

Safe Horizon is the largest provider of domestic violence services in the country. Collaborating with the criminal justice system, Safe Horizon offers innovative programs that provide women with support throughout the complex process of leaving violent relationships and building safe futures.

Victoria Family Violence Prevention Society
2541 Empire Street
Victoria, BC V8T 3M3
Canada
(250) 380-1955
E-mail: fvp@familyviolence.ca
Web site: http://www.familyviolence.ca/splash.htm
This organization works to end violence and abuse in intimate relationships.

Web Sites

Due to the changing nature of Internet links, the Rosen Publishing Group, Inc., has developed an online list of Web sites related to the subject of this book. This site is updated regularly. Please use this link to access the list:

http://www.rosenlinks.com/vas/dovi

FOR FURTHER READING

Brown, Isobel. *Domestic Crime*. Broomall, PA: Mason Crest Publishers, 2002.

Feuereisen, Patti, and Caroline Pincus. *Invisible Girls: The Truth About Sexual Abuse*. New York, NY: Seal Press, 2005.

Landau, Elaine. *Date Violence*. New York, NY: Scholastic Library Publishing, 2004.

Levy, Barrie. *In Love and in Danger: A Teen's Guide to Breaking Free of Abusive Relationships*. New York, NY: Avalon Publishing Group, 2006.

Mintzer, Richard. *Coping with Random Acts of Violence*. New York, NY: Rosen Publishing Group, 2004.

Roleff, Tamara. *Domestic Violence*. Farmington Hills, MI: Gale Group, 2000.

Shellenberger, Susie. *How to Help Your Hurting Friend: Clear Guidance for Messy Problems*. Grand Rapids, MI: Zondervan, 2004.

Stark, Evan. *Everything You Need to Know About Family Violence*. New York, NY: Rosen Publishing Group, 2000.

Yount, Lisa. *How Can Domestic Violence Be Prevented?* Farmington Hills, MI: Gale Group, 2006.

Yuwiler, Janice M. *Family Violence*. Farmington Hills, MI: Gale Group, 2004.

ABC News. "Confession Released in Nixzmary Case." *Eyewitness News,* 2006. Retrieved November 1, 2007 (http://abclocal. go.com/wabc/story?section = local&id = 4788924).

ABC News. "New Details in Tortured New York Girl's Death." January 18, 2006. Retrieved November 1, 2007 (http:// abcnews.go.com/US/LegalCenter/story?id = 1517137).

American Bar Association. "Domestic Violence: Safety Tips for You and Your Family." Retrieved November 1, 2007 (http://www.abanet.org/tips/dvsafety.html).

Berry, Dawn Bradley. *The Domestic Violence Sourcebook.* New York, NY: McGraw-Hill, 2000.

Brick, Michael. "Reporters Won't Have to Testify in Death." *New York Times,* September 13, 2007. Retrieved November 1, 2007 (http://www.nytimes.com/2007/09/13/nyregion/ 13girl.html?_r = 2&oref = slogin&oref = slogin).

British Broadcasting Corporation. "Domestic Violence—Men as Victims." December 2005. Retrieved November 12, 2007 (http://www.bbc.co.uk/relationships/domestic_violence/ menhh_index.shtml).

Campbell, Bob. "Child Murders Not a Modern Phenomenon, but Society Is Getting Tougher in Response." MyWestTexas.com, September 4, 2005. Retrieved November 20, 2007 (http:// www.mywesttexas.com/site/news.cfm?newsid = 15153412).

CBS News. "Outrage Over Abuse, Death of NYC Girl." *CBS Early Show,* January 13, 2006. Retrieved November 1, 2007 (http://www.cbsnews.com/stories/2006/01/13/earlyshow/ main1206722.shtml).

Center for the Improvement of Child Caring. "Corporal Punishment and Verbal Aggression." Retrieved November 1, 2007 (http://www.ciccparenting.org/NewsLetters/ corporalpunishment.htm).

CNN. "Nancy Grace Transcript: Airing January 19, 2006." 2007. Retrieved November 1, 2007 (http://transcripts.cnn.com/TRANSCRIPTS/0601/19/ng.01.html).

Commissioner for Human Rights, Council of Europe. "Children and Corporal Punishment: The Right Not to Be Hit, Also a Children's Right." Updated September 18, 2006. Retrieved November 1, 2007 (http://www.crin.org/resources/infoDetail.asp?ID = 8562&flag = report).

Committee on the Rights of the Child. "The Convention on the Rights of the Child and Its Treaty Body." Retrieved November 1, 2007 (http://www.endcorporalpunishment.org/pages/hrlaw/crc_session.html).

Department of Justice/Federal Bureau of Investigation. "Violent Crime." Updated February 17, 2006. Retrieved November 1, 2007 (http://www.fbi.gov/ucr/cius_04/offenses_reported/violent_crime/index.html).

Family Doctor.org Editorial Staff. "Domestic Violence: Protecting Yourself and Your Children." American Academy of Family Physicians, April 2005. Retrieved November 1, 2007 (http://familydoctor.org/online/famdocen/home/healthy/safety/kids-family/052.printerview.html).

HelpGuide.org. "Domestic Violence and Abuse." August 20, 2007. Retrieved November 1, 2007 (http://www.helpguide.org/mental/domestic_violence_abuse_types_signs_causes_effects.htm).

Kaufman, Leslie, Mike McIntire, and Fernanda Santos. "Child Welfare Offices That Couldn't Be Fixed Fast Enough." *New York Times*, January 20, 2006. Retrieved November 1, 2007 (http://www.nytimes.com/2006/01/20/nyregion/20child.html).

Mayo Clinic. "Domestic Violence Towards Women: Recognize the Patterns and Seek Help." May 23, 2007. Retrieved November 1, 2007 (http://www.mayoclinic.com/health/domestic-violence/WO00044).

Medline Plus. "Domestic Violence." November 10, 2007. Retrieved November 1, 2007 (http://www.nlm.nih.gov/medlineplus/domesticviolence.html).

National Center for Victims of Crime. "Domestic Violence." 1999. Retrieved November 1, 2007 (http://www.ncvc.org/ncvc/main.aspx?dbName=DocumentViewer&DocumentID=32347).

National Domestic Violence Hotline. "Safety Planning." 1998. Retrieved November 1, 2007 (http://www.ndvh.org/help/planning.html).

Nemours Foundation. Reviewed by Michelle New, PhD. "Abuse." November 2007. Retrieved November 1, 2007 (http://kidshealth.org/teen/your_mind/families/family_abuse.html).

Schornstein, Sherri Lynn. *Domestic Violence and Health Care: What Every Professional Needs to Know*. Washington, DC: Sage Publications, 1997.

USA Today. "Final Days of Girl's Life Reveal Horrors." January 21, 2007. Retrieved November 1, 2007 (http://www.usatoday.com/news/nation/2006-01-21-child-death_x.htm).

U.S. Department of Justice, Bureau of Justice Statistics. "Intimate Partner Violence in the United States." December 2006. Retrieved January 7, 2008 (http://www.ojp.usdoj.gov/bjs/intimate/ipv.htm).

INDEX

About the Author

Holly Cefrey is an award-winning author of books for children and teens. She graduated from New York University with a specialized degree in nonfiction writing. She enjoys writing books that empower youth and help them to cope with confusing and difficult issues.

Photo Credits

Cover (left) Kay Blaschke/Stock4B/Getty Images; cover (right) © www.istockphoto.com/Jason Stitt; cover, back cover (background) © www.istockphoto.com/Stefan Klein; p. 4 Spencer Platt/Getty Images; pp. 7, 27 © AP Images; p. 9 © Peter Marlow/Magnum Photos; p. 12 Rob Schoenbaum/Time & Life Pictures/Getty Images; p. 16 © www.istockphoto.com/Galina Barskaya; p. 18 © Susan Meiselas/Magnum Photos; pp. 20, 35 © Esbin-Anderson/The Image Works; p. 23 © www.istockphoto.com/ericsphotography; pp. 24, 29 © Bob Daemmrich/The Image Works; p. 25 © The British Library/Topham-HIP/The Image Works; p. 32 © John Birdsall/The Image Works; p. 39 © Journal-Courier/Tiffany M. Hermon/The Image Works; p. 42 © Christina Kennedy/DK Stock/Getty Images; p. 45 © Zigy Kaluzny/Stone/Getty Images; p. 47 © www.istockphoto.com/Robert Churchill; p. 49 © Mark Antman/The Image Works.

Designer: Nelson Sá; **Editor:** Christopher Roberts
Photo Researcher: Cindy Reiman